To: _____

From: _____

Louis Weber, CEO
Publications International, Ltd.
7373 North Cicero Avenue
Lincolnwood, Illinois 60712

**www.pilbooks.com**

Manufactured in China.

8 7 6 5 4 3 2 1

ISBN: 978-1-4508-9923-9

# Mothers & Daughters

## Why daughters always need their mothers

Written by Meredith R. Katz

new seasons®

# A daughter needs a mother...

...to guide her through the steps of childhood.

A daughter needs a mother...

...to give her an extra boost
in the obstacle course of life.

A daughter needs a mother...

...who will give her the courage to take risks.

# A daughter needs a mother...

...to share secret family recipes.

# A daughter needs a mother...

...so she knows the meaning of unconditional love.

A daughter needs a mother...

...to show her how even the smallest
act can help change the world.

*A daughter needs a mother...*

...to teach her what it means to share.

...to be her rock when times are hard.

A daughter needs a mother...

...to remind her how sweet life truly is.

# A daughter needs a mother...

…who takes pride in the strength of her family.

A daughter needs a mother...

...who will give her comfort no
matter what kind of storm she is facing.

A daughter needs a mother...

…who will remind her to take a jacket
— even when she's grown.

A daughter needs a mother...

...who can soothe her heart with
wise words and a gentle touch.

...who makes every milestone all the more meaningful.

# A daughter needs a mother...

...who nourishes her body <u>and</u> her soul.

A daughter needs a mother...

...to show her that making the journey is more important than reaching the destination.

A daughter needs a mother...

…who is happy to share her company,
regardless of what she is doing.

# A daughter needs a mother...

...to teach her the meaning of sisterhood.

A daughter needs a mother...

...to bring out the laughter no one else can.

…who will teach her the etiquette she needs
to become a young lady.

A daughter needs a mother...

...to show her where she comes from
and who she may become.

# A daughter needs a mother...

...to teach her when to hold on tight and when to let go.

A daughter needs a mother...

…who will encourage her to let her imagination run wild.

A daughter needs a mother...

...who will teach her how to be streetwise,
for the days she must travel alone.

A daughter needs a mother...

...to help her acquire the knowledge she will need to face the world on her own.

A daughter needs a mother...

...to teach her the importance of a little pampering.

A daughter needs a mother...

...who is a constant source of support and strength.

A daughter needs a mother...

…who encourages her to take the
first big steps toward her future.

A daughter needs a mother...

...to remind her that self worth is based
on much more than a pretty face.

A daughter needs a mother...

...who will show her that there's always time to dance.

# A daughter needs a mother...

...to teach her the importance of tradition.

# A daughter needs a mother...

...to be the wisest teacher she'll ever have.

A daughter needs a mother...

…who will never think she's too old to need her.

# A daughter needs a mother...

...so she knows one person will always handle her heart with care.

# A daughter needs a mother...

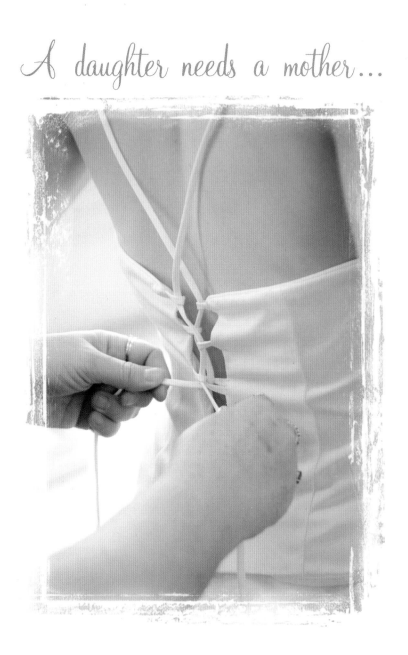

...to stand by her on the most important day of her life.

A daughter needs a mother...

…with whom she can share her secrets and dreams.